The Book Rescuer

A note on the subtitle: *Mensch* is the English version of the Yiddish word *mentsh*, which means person. Though the transliterated spelling, *mentsh*, is often used, the author and publisher decided to use the more familiar spelling in this book. In English, we use *mensch* to mean a person of good character.

The publisher gratefully acknowledges Dr. Asya Vaisman Schulman, the director of the Yiddish Language Institute at the Yiddish Book Center, for her expert review of the Yiddish in this book.

SIMON & SCHUSTER BOOKS FOR YOUNG READERS
An imprint of Simon & Schuster Children's Publishing Division
1230 Avenue of the Americas, New York, New York 10020
Text copyright © 2019 by Sue Macy
Illustrations copyright © 2019 by Stacy Innerst
All rights reserved, including the right of reproduction in whole or in part in any form.
SIMON & SCHUSTER BOOKS FOR YOUNG READERS
is a trademark of Simon & Schuster, Inc.
For information about special discounts for bulk purchases, please contact
Simon & Schuster Special Sales at 1-866-506-1949 or business@simonandschuster.com.
The Simon & Schuster Speakers Bureau can bring authors to your live event.
For more information or to book an event, contact the Simon & Schuster Speakers Bureau
at 1-866-248-3049 or visit our website at www.simonspeakers.com.
Book design by Laurent Linn
The text for this book was set in Bitstream Carmina BT.
The illustrations for this book were rendered in acrylic and gouache
on gessoed illustration board, with fabric textures added digitally.
Manufactured in China
0719 SCP
First Edition
2 4 6 8 10 9 7 5 3 1
Library of Congress Cataloging-in-Publication Data
Names: Macy, Sue, author. | Innerst, Stacy, illustrator.
Title: The book rescuer, : how a mensch from Massachusetts saved Yiddish literature for generations
to come / by Sue Macy ; illustrated by Stacy Innerst.
Description: First edition. | New York : Simon & Schuster, [2019] | Ages 5–8, K to grade 3.
Identifiers: LCCN 2018040581| ISBN 9781481472203 (hardcover) | ISBN 9781481472210 (eBook)
Subjects: LCSH: Lansky, Aaron, 1955——Juvenile literature. | Book collectors—Massachusetts—New
Bedford—Biography—Juvenile literature. | Jewish men—Massachusetts—New Bedford—Biography—Juvenile
literature. | National Yiddish Book Center (U.S.)—History—Juvenile literature. |
Yiddish language—Revival—Juvenile literature.
Classification: LCC Z989.L36 M33 2019 | DDC 020.75 [B]—dc23
LC record available at https://lccn.loc.gov/2018040581

The Book Rescuer

How a Mensch from Massachusetts Saved
Yiddish Literature for Generations to Come

WRITTEN BY
SUE MACY

ILLUSTRATED BY
STACY INNERST

A Paula Wiseman Book

SIMON & SCHUSTER
BOOKS FOR YOUNG READERS

New York   London   Toronto   Sydney   New Delhi

Kum aher. Sit down. I want to tell you a story. It starts a long time ago, when Aaron Lansky's sixteen-year-old grandma left Eastern Europe for the United States. She didn't bring much with her. Just a cardboard suitcase with some precious items from her old life. A goose-down pillow. A pair of candlesticks. A photograph of her mama and papa, who stayed in Europe. And a few books in Yiddish, the everyday language of Eastern European Jews.

After a long ocean voyage, Aaron's grandma reached New York City, where her older brother was waiting. He greeted her, took the suitcase, and tossed it into the Hudson River. *Oy, gevald!* He said it was time to break with the past—and think about the future.

Aaron never forgot that story. Who could? It made him curious about the life his grandma left behind. Make no mistake, Aaron was an all-American boy. He grew up in New Bedford, Massachusetts, horsing around with his two brothers. He joined the Boy Scouts. He watched *Star Trek*.

He also loved books. Aaron received his first library card at age four. From that time forward, he read everything he could get his hands on.

Is it a surprise, then, that books would end up playing a big part in Aaron's life? Of course not. In college he decided to study Jewish history by reading novels written by Jews of the past. He felt they were the perfect way to understand how Jewish people lived. But many of the books Aaron wanted to read were written in Yiddish. So *nu*, first he had to learn the language.

During the early decades of the twentieth century, as many as thirteen million people around the world spoke Yiddish. By the time Aaron was growing up in the 1960s, though, Yiddish was *af tsores*—in trouble. Nazi Germany and its allies killed millions of Yiddish-speaking Jews in World War II, from 1939 to 1945. Other Yiddish speakers fled Eastern Europe and raised their children in countries where they learned the local languages instead of Yiddish.

maven

מֵבִין

Mazel Tov!

מַזָּל-טוֹב

Kosher

כָּשֵׁר

Schmooze

שְׁמוּעַס

SCH

עפ

Plotz

פְּלַאץ

NOSH

נאַש

Although Aaron was the grandson of Eastern European immigrants, he knew only those Yiddish words that had entered the English language. Words like "bagel" and "klutz" and "nosh" and "glitch." "No one ever spoke Yiddish to me, to my brothers, or to anyone else our age," he said. Like many other first-generation American Jews, Aaron's parents wanted their *kinder* to fit in by speaking and reading English.

BAGEL
בייגל

LEP
של

schmutz
שמוץ

KLUTZ
קלאץ

GLITCH
גליטש

As Yiddish speakers disappeared, so did books written in Yiddish. Students like Aaron had a hard time finding Yiddish books for school. That's why he was stunned when he visited his hometown rabbi and spotted a basket filled with Yiddish books on the floor of his office. What were they doing there? The rabbi said he intended to bury them.

Aaron could have plotzed! Destroying Yiddish books was like erasing Jewish history! But these books were no longer useful, the rabbi explained, and burying them was a sign of respect. Aaron was not having it. With the rabbi's blessing, he took everything in the basket.

Aaron said Yiddish books were the "portable homeland" of the Jewish people. What did he mean by that? Before the founding of Israel in 1948, Jews didn't have their own homeland. Instead, they lived in countries all over the world. It was through books that Jews recorded and shared their experiences and beliefs. "Books are big enough and powerful enough to define and contain identity," said Aaron.

Aaron's search for Yiddish books continued in Montreal, Canada, where he had started graduate school. Soon he was flooded with donations. He collected so many books that he could hardly find room to sleep in his apartment. *Vey iz mir.* At the same time, his parents said their house was getting crowded with baskets of books from Aaron's rabbi. They were starting to worry that the second story would collapse from the added weight!

As the books piled up, Aaron realized he was no longer interested in simply gathering enough for his own use. Now he wanted to save as many Yiddish books as possible. So what did he do? I'll tell you. He took time off from graduate school and hauled his entire library back to Massachusetts.

Then he went to see the leaders of the biggest Jewish organizations in the country. "If we don't save these books now, they'll be lost *forever*," Aaron told them. But the leaders shook their heads. They said Yiddish was a language whose time had passed.

Fortunately, Aaron wouldn't take no for an answer.
He rented space in an old factory building and founded
the Yiddish Book Center, dedicated to collecting unwanted
Yiddish books. After a reporter from the *Boston Globe* wrote
an article about the center, boxes of books started to arrive.

So did frantic phone calls. One particular call came at midnight from a friend of Aaron's in New York City. She had found a dumpster full of Yiddish books, she said, and it was scheduled to be hauled off to the trash heap later that day. What's more, the weather forecasters were predicting rain.

It was snowing in Massachusetts that night and the roads were icy, but Aaron rushed to the railroad station to catch the two a.m. train to New York.

As the sun rose and the rain fell, Aaron and a group of friends rummaged through the giant garbage container. It was filled with thousands of books, emptied out of a nearby building that had once housed a Yiddish organization. Aaron and his buddies managed to get close to five thousand of them into a rented truck, which he drove all the way home.

Aaron also set out on less hazardous trips to collect books offered up by older Jews. He drove to houses and apartments in New York, New Jersey, Pennsylvania, and beyond. The people he visited called him *yunger-man*—young man—and plied him with food as they shared their stories. Over tea and cake and *lokshn kugl*, they told Aaron about their jobs, their families, their communities.

Most of all, they told him about their books. These men and women handed Aaron one book at a time, their eyes filling with tears as they recounted when they bought it and what it meant to them. "We didn't eat much," one woman told Aaron, "but we always bought a book. It was a necessity of life."

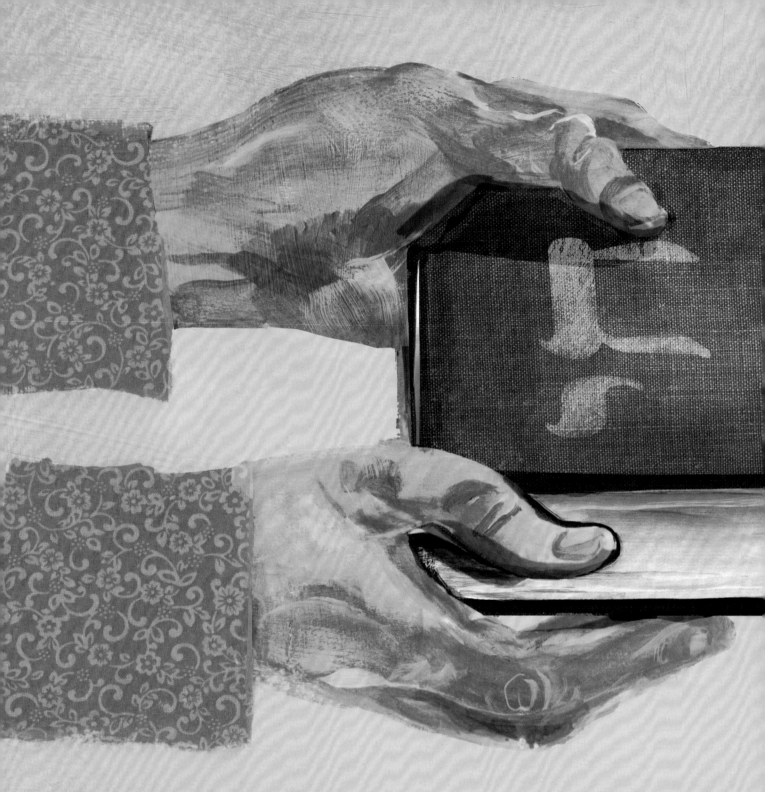

Aaron felt their sadness at having no family members who could read their prized possessions. And he saw their relief once they realized they could trust him to keep their books safe.

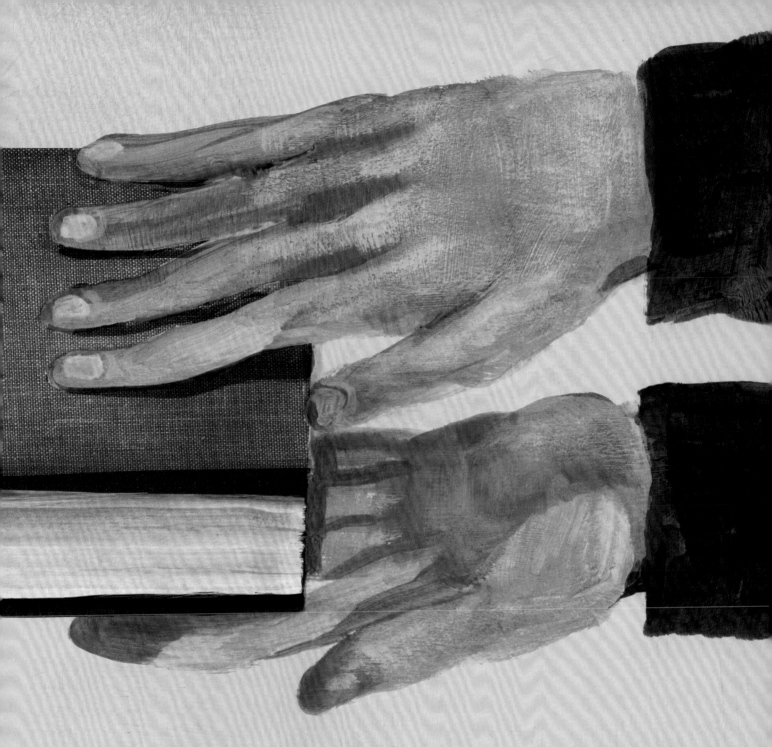

When Aaron founded the Yiddish Book Center in 1980, experts believed there might be only seventy thousand Yiddish books left in the world. He collected that many in six months—and kept going. And wouldn't you know it, people started paying attention. In 1989, Aaron won an award known as a MacArthur "genius grant," given to people who make a difference in the world. The MacArthur Foundation praised Aaron for giving Yiddish culture new life and introducing it to new generations.

Aaron's accomplishments certainly would have made his grandma *kvel*. Although the suitcase she brought to New York is long gone, Aaron has kept her story alive by saving a million and a half Yiddish books. But the books don't just sit around collecting dust. Aaron shares them with schools and libraries and uses them in programs about Yiddish literature. "Between their covers," he said, "the voices of my grandmother's world can still be heard."

Aaron Lansky at his desk in the Yiddish Book Center's earlier location, known as East Street School, in Amherst, Massachusetts, in 1982.

Aaron Lansky at the Yiddish Book Center in 2011.

AFTERWORD

by
AARON LANSKY

I WAS TWENTY-FOUR YEARS OLD WHEN I FIRST EMBARKED ON the adventures described in this book. What have my colleagues and I been doing in the almost four decades since?

Well, we're *still* collecting books, which is amazing when you consider that it's been almost a century since Congress cut off mass Jewish immigration to America. Somehow boxes of Yiddish books still arrive every day, and we're still heading out on the road to find more. Next week, for example, we're off for Poland, where the only known copy of Isaac Bashevis Singer's first literary work recently surfaced in his hometown of Bilgoraj.

It's one thing to rescue Yiddish books; it's quite another to get people to read them. Twenty years ago we decided to digitize our titles, and ten years ago we placed them online, available for free to anyone who wanted to read them. Would you believe they've since been downloaded more than two and a half *million* times, often by younger readers who learned Yiddish in college?

Forty-three people work with me at the Yiddish Book Center nowadays. We're racing against time to save Jews' stories as well as their books. We're training a new generation of Yiddish translators. We're releasing a new textbook that will make learning Yiddish quicker, easier, and more fun. And we're offering exciting educational programs for high school students, college students, twenty-somethings, and adults.

I'll admit it: Racing around in a rattletrap truck in search of dusty books was a lot of fun. But what we're doing now—opening up those books, excavating the lost civilization they contain, and sharing its treasures with the world—that's even better. After all these years I can't wait to see what happens next.

AUTHOR'S NOTE

IF YOU WALKED DOWN ANY STREET ON THE LOWER EAST SIDE of New York City at the beginning of the twentieth century, your ears would be bombarded with Yiddish. Peddlers hawking their goods, customers haggling for better prices, parents yelling for their kids to come in to dinner would all be speaking Yiddish. More than two million Jews immigrated to the United States from 1881 to 1924, and Yiddish was the main language many of them spoke. They gave rise to a vibrant Yiddish press—with 150 Yiddish newspapers and periodicals debuting by 1914 in New York alone—as well as a lively Yiddish theater scene and, in the 1930s, a healthy offering of Yiddish radio programs.

Today there are only about 150,000 people who speak Yiddish at home in the United States. Many are Hasidic Jews, following ultra-Orthodox religious practices and using the language to separate from the mainstream. Others are "heritage speakers," elderly Jews who grew up speaking Yiddish or younger ones who heard it in their homes. There is also a small but growing number of people actively studying Yiddish in the United States and Europe. Some of them are nonreligious Jews who see the language as a way to connect with their history and culture. But there are also non-Jews who are passionate about the language and its literature.

Thanks to the Yiddish Book Center, people learning Yiddish today and those interested in Yiddish literature have plenty of resources. The center has uploaded more than eleven thousand adult books and more than eight hundred children's books from its collection, offering them for free to interested readers on its website, yiddishbookcenter.org. The site also features Yiddish and English oral history videos, audiobooks in Yiddish, and lectures given by Yiddish writers that were recorded as far back as 1935 (some in English, others in Yiddish). The center continues to produce translations of books and stories so English speakers can access some of the material as well.

ILLUSTRATOR'S NOTE

THE PICTURES IN THIS BOOK WERE INSPIRED BY THE extraordinary vision of Marc Chagall. There is, perhaps, no painter who conveyed the visual language of his culture more intimately and poetically than Chagall, and I've loved his work for as long as I can remember. He was born in 1887 in Vitebsk, Russia, to a poor, Orthodox Jewish family. His success as a modern painter took him all over the world, including the art centers of Paris and New York, yet the exuberant motifs of his compositions were steeped in the characters and architecture of his early life in the shtetl.

I had the good fortune to grow up in a home with people who appreciated great art and literature and whose walls were lined with books. My mother was a librarian and my father a journalist and writer. Of particular interest to me was a set of tiny books called The Pocket Library of Great Art, which were full of color plates of paintings by Klee, Dufy, Utrillo, Cézanne, Rouault, and of course, Marc Chagall.

Those books were my touchstone for what painting could be and the images that I pored over as a child filled my uncluttered mind with color, form, and pure expression. Chagall, in particular, showed me a fantastic world that was unbound by time, space, or gravity, and yet still very accessible and human.

As an illustrator of picture book biographies, I have the opportunity to become a student of a vast array of subjects and personalities. My favorite part of the research process is discovering and finding inspiration in the world that I'm attempting to illustrate. When I first read the manuscript for this book and was introduced to Aaron Lansky's noble mission, I realized that I had some catching up to do. I had very little knowledge of Yiddish culture or history, and what little I knew was from the life depicted in Chagall's swirling paintings.

So . . . I went back to the beginning and to the Pocket Library. It was right where I had left it.

Thank goodness there are people in this world that keep—and sometimes rescue—books.

GLOSSARY OF YIDDISH WORDS AND EXPRESSIONS

In this book, Yiddish words that have entered the English language, such as bagel and nosh, are not in italics. That includes all the words on pages 16-17. Those words are shown alongside their spellings in Yiddish characters. When you see words in italics, they are transliterations of Yiddish, meaning they use the closest corresponding English letters to show a word from the Yiddish language. For example, *oy, gevald* is the transliteration of אוי, געוואַלד.

af tsores: in trouble (page 15)

bagel: English word meaning a donut-shaped bread, which comes from the Yiddish word *beygl* (page 17)

glitch: English version of the Yiddish word *glitsh*, which means slip or slippery conditions; in English a glitch refers to a malfunction (page 17)

kinder: children (page 17)

klutz: English word meaning a clumsy person, which comes from the Yiddish word *klots* (literally, "a block of wood") (page 17)

kosher: English word of Yiddish origin, designating that food satisfies Jewish dietary laws; also used to describe something that is satisfactory or legitimate (page 16)

kum aher: come here (page 7)

kvel: beam with pride (page 36)

lokshn kugl: noodle pudding (page 32)

maven: English word meaning an expert, which comes from the Yiddish word *meyvn* (page 16)

mazel tov: English term, used to express congratulations, which comes from the Yiddish *mazl-tov* (page 16)

mensch: English word meaning a person of good character, which comes from the Yiddish word *mentsh*, meaning person (title page)

nosh: snack (page 16)

nu: well, so (usually phrased as a question) (page 12)

44

oy, gevald!: good grief! (page 8)

plotz: English word meaning to be beside oneself or overcome with emotion, which comes from the Yiddish word *plats*, meaning to burst or explode (page 16)

schlep: English word meaning drag or haul, which comes from the Yiddish word *shlep* (pages 16-17)

schmooze: English word meaning chat or gossip, which comes from the Yiddish word *shmues* (page 16)

schmutz: English word meaning dirt, which comes from the Yiddish word *shmuts* (page 17)

vey iz mir: woe is me (page 22)

yunger-man: young man (page 32)

Note: Yiddish books, like Hebrew books, are written and read from right to left. The spines of the books are on the right. Compared to books in English, they are read back to front.

The book on pages 34–35 says "khay," which means "life" in Hebrew, but can be used in Yiddish as well.

Outwitting History: The Amazing Adventures of a Man Who Rescued a Million Yiddish Books by Aaron Lansky (Chapel Hill, NC: Algonquin Books of Chapel Hill, 2004).

Written for adults, Aaron Lansky's memoir is as entertaining as it is informative. Read it for a firsthand look at the excitement and challenges of preserving Yiddish books—and, through them, the history and culture of Eastern European Jews.

Yiddish Book Center, 1021 West Street, Amherst, MA 01002; phone: 413-256-4900; website: www.yiddishbookcenter.org.

If you visit New England, the Yiddish Book Center is definitely worth a stop. You'll find gardens dedicated to Yiddish writers, exhibits on Jewish history and culture, an original Yiddish printing press from the *Forverts (Forward)* daily newspaper, sheet music for Yiddish songs, and a library with lots and lots of books. If you can't go in person, or even if you can, be sure to check out the center's website. It will keep you busy for days.

The Yiddish Book Center in Amherst, Massachusetts.

SOURCE NOTES

HERE ARE THE SOURCES OF SPECIFIC QUOTES
AND STATISTICS USED IN THE BOOK.

PAGE 15: "as many as thirteen million . . .": "Language: Yiddish," by Dovid Katz, *The YIVO Encyclopedia of Jews in Eastern Europe*, YIVO Institute for Jewish Research, 2010, accessed January 30, 2019, at http://www.yivoencyclopedia.org/article.aspx/Language/Yiddish.

PAGE 17: "'No one ever . . . our age'": Aaron Lansky, *Outwitting History: The Amazing Adventures of a Man Who Rescued a Million Yiddish Books*, Chapel Hill, Algonquin Books of Chapel Hill, 2005 paperback, p. 9.

PAGE 21: "'portable homeland'" and "Books are . . . identity": Nancy Wolfson-Moche, "Aaron Lansky," in *Jewish Sages of Today: Profiles of Extraordinary People*, edited by Aryeh Rubin (New York: Devora Publishing, 2009), p. 103. Accessed October 4, 2017, at https://www.yumpu.com/en/document/view/5721540/aaron-lansky-jewish-sages-of-today.

PAGE 25: "If we don't . . . *forever*": Lansky, *Outwitting History*, p. 49.

PAGE 26: "founded the Yiddish Book Center": Lansky, *Outwitting History*, p. 47. Note: Aaron first named his organization the National Yiddish Book Exchange, but he changed the name to the National Yiddish Book Center two years later. Although that is still the official name, "National" was dropped from the center's logo in 2011.

PAGE 33: "We didn't eat much . . . life": Clara Krugman, quoted in Douglas C. McGill, "Literary Labor of Love Is Saving Yiddish Books," *New York Times*, July 25, 1983.

PAGE 36: "'Between . . . be heard'": Lansky, *Outwitting History*, p. 302.

PAGE 42: "More than two million Jews immigrated . . .": "Eastern European Immigrants in the United States," by Paula E. Hyman, Jewish Women's Archive. Accessed October 16, 2018, at https://jwa.org/encyclopedia/article/eastern-european-immigrants-in-united-states.

PAGE 42: "Yiddish was the main language . . .": Sol Steinmetz, *Yiddish and English: The Story of Yiddish in America*, 2nd ed. (Tuscaloosa: University of Alabama Press, 2001), p. 17.

PAGE 42: "150 Yiddish newspapers . . .": Steinmetz, *Yiddish and English*, p. 18.

PAGE 42: "only about 150,000 . . .": 2011 update to the 2007 American Community Survey on Language Use, quoted in Tanya Basu, *"Oy Vey: Yiddish Has a Problem," The Atlantic*, September 9, 2014. Accessed April 5, 2018, at https://www.theatlantic.com/national/archive/2014/09/yiddish-has-a-problem/379658/.

ACKNOWLEDGMENTS

I COULD NOT HAVE WRITTEN this book without the help and support of the folks at the Yiddish Book Center, starting with founder Aaron Lansky and director of communications Lisa Newman. I appreciate their willingness to sit for interviews, correct my word usage, and generally encourage me every step of the way.

As always, thanks to my wise and patient editor, Sylvie Frank, and the rest of the team at Paula Wiseman Books. They were the ones who brought award-winning illustrator Stacy Innerst on to this project, and I couldn't be more thrilled. Thank you for your elegant work, Stacy! Thanks also to Amanda Seigel, librarian at the Dorot Jewish Division of the New York Public Library and a celebrated performer of Yiddish music, who graciously gave me an overview of the state of Yiddish in the United States today. *A groysn dank.* Thank you very much.

Finally, thanks to my mom and my late grandmother for inspiring me to write this book by providing an ongoing soundtrack of Yiddish conversation through-out my childhood.

—S. M.

A PROFOUND THANK-YOU to author, Sue Macy; editor, Sylvie Frank; and everyone at Paula Wiseman Books—especially all-around *mensch*, Laurent Linn, for his insight and guidance.

Thanks also to my polyglot brother, Ivan, for his encouragement along the way.

—S. I.